D1555752

We Have Our Voice

Selected Poems of

Reesom Haile

ደሃይና እሎ፞ና

ም፞ሩጽ ግጥም፞ታት ርእሶም ሃይለ

English Translations with
Charles Cantalupo

The Red Sea Press, Inc.

Publishers & Distributors of Third World Books

11-D Princess Road   P. O. Box 48
Lawrenceville, NJ 08648   Asmara, ERITREA

The Red Sea Press, Inc.

Publishers & Distributors of Third World Books

11-D Princess Road  P. O. Box 48
Lawrenceville, NJ 08648 Asmara, ERITREA

Copyright © 2000 Reesom Haile and Charles Cantalupo

First Printing 2000

Book Design: Wanjiku Ngugi & Elias Amaré Gebrezgheir
Cover Design: Yegizaw Michael
Cover and Book Illustrations and Art: Yegizaw Michael

Library of Congress Cataloging-in-Publication Data

Reesom Haile.
 [Poems. English & Tigrinya. Selections]
 We have our voice: selected poems of Ressom Haile - Dhayna
'alona : merus getemtat Re'esom Hayla / English translations with
Charles Cantalupo.
 p. cm.
 ISBN 1-56902-132-5 (cloth) -- ISBN 1-56902-133-3 (paperback)
 1. Reesom Haile--Translations into English. I. Cantalupo,
Charles, 1951- II. Title.

PJ9111.9.R442 A23 2000
892'.831--dc21   99-045185

The Tigrinya poems in this volume first appeared in *Waza ms Qum Neger n Tensae Hager* first published in 1997 in the US by Yohana Mahtem, copyright © 1997 Resseom Haile; and in *Bahlna Bahlbna*, published by Francescana Printing, Asmara, December 1999, copyright © 1999 Reesom Haile. The publisher is grateful to the author and Yohana Mahtem for permission to reprint the Tigrinya poems in this volume. Poems from this volume have also appeared in *About.com*, *Left Curve* and the *Light and Dust Anthology of Poetry*.

Dedication   ወፈያ

≪ንሃገሮም/ንሃገረን ህይወቶም/ህይወተን ዘሕለፉ/ዘሕለፋ
ንሃገሮም/ንሃገረን ናጽነት ዘትረፉ/ዘትረፋ።≫

To the
" . . . men and women
Who sacrifice[d] their lives.
We have a nation."

Contents

Preface

I first encountered Reesom Haile in Asmara, one evening during Eritrea's annual, outdoor, 8-day cultural festival: a highly popular event, thronged with people from Asmara and from throughout Eritrea, and featuring all of the arts—agricultural, domestic, industrial, language, performing, technological, visual. Taking place in the extensive fairgrounds called "Expo," the festival's theme was "Inheritance." It encouraged Eritreans from all walks of life to taste and see their new nation through the many forms of its longstanding and highly valued multicultural and multimedia expression. Be it a poem, a computer program, a painting, an ancient manuscript, a display of tools, a dance, desert housing, a popular song, a camel, a coffee, a textile or a pile of particular wood to make a fire, people could look all around them at a wealth of highly varied examples of their culture, including each other, and marvel, "We have...we have...we have."

I was following the crowd to a poetry reading. The area where it took place seemed to be shaped like a basin, with children—whom I didn't expect to see at such an event—seated in the middle, the poet and the audience at opposite edges. Actually, the arrangement was just a platform with a podium and the audience gathered in a flat place in front of it—but my initial misimpression was telling.

Amiri Baraka, the poet of my home soil, Newark, New Jersey, has written that

> [t]he arts are not peripheral to human development but at the center of it....They are education, information, inspiration and economic development, if someone would but recognize it....It's up to us, the artists, to take up thechallenge and not leave it.... [A]rt is to raise the people, the artists must take it upon themselves.

The Expo festival put "the arts...at the center" in a way that I had never realized—because it included so many different kinds of arts and people—and never experienced before. However, when Reesom Haile read his poems, I saw "Art...raise the people" again as I had never witnessed. The audience and the reading space seemed physically raised up to be even with the poet speaking his lines. The children in the middle were joining Reesom Haile in his lines, anticipating and echoing them, with great pleasure, too, especially when he spoke the poem, "Alowuna, Alowana," "We Have." It swept through the crowd and it was sweeping the entire nation and its diaspora with the verbal music of Tigrinya affirmation:

> We have men and women...
> We have women and men....
> Without end in the struggle
> To grow, study and persist.
> Who think and think again
> To teach, learn and know...
> Without the lust for power.
> Who stand up or down
> With our consent.
> We have God and a future.
> We have men and women
> Who belong in our nation
> And we belong with them....
> We have women and men.
> Rejoice.

"Rejoice." I say it again when poetry can become a kind of daily bread or currency for all kinds of people—writers, children, artists, young professionals, working people, the elderly, government people —and create a rapport and a give and take among all, including the poet. This is a work of high value.

Poet and scholar, Reesom Haile has returned to Eritrea after a twenty-year exile, which included teaching in Communications at The New School for Social Research in New York and a subsequent career as a Development Communications Consultant, working with UN Agencies, governments and NGOs around the world.

He is widely recognized for his revolutionary modernization of the traditional art of poetry in Tigrinya, one of Eritrea's main languages. We Have Our Voice is the first bilingual collection of his poetry. Its enormous popular appeal—in print and on the internet —spills into the streets of Asmara and the rest of Eritrea, where to stroll with Reesom Haile at any hour is to be approached by the young and old and all kinds of people who are delighted to quote his lines back to him. Reesom Haile explains the phenomenon this way:

> Our poetry is not something that has left our tongue and lived in the books for a very long time. Our poetry is participatory. When I recite my poetry at home, the people listening to me will say, "add this to that, add this to that." It is participatory. It's not something that we put on the wall and say "Oh, this is pretty." Our traditional poetry form is ad hoc. Someone will just get up and say something to try to capture the spirit of that particular time. And people will add, "why don't you say so, why don't you add this, why don't you extend it." It is very much part of the tradition. I am putting it on paper because I think it is about time we start storing it for the next generation.

Thus a poet, almost by necessity an individualist, can also be a voice of the people and a kind of nationalist, albeit spontaneously through the construction of a parallel between tradition and change: in John Coltrane's words, "a force for real good." It illuminates within *We Have Our Voice*, only a small selection of Reesom Haile's work, a wide variety of topics, including gender equality, colonialism, foreign aid, the use of knowledge, bureaucracy, history, crime, priests, travel, daughters and sons, sisters and brothers, camels, books, education, homecomings, exile, money, computers, braggarts, religion, political leadership, hopes, delusions, bravery, civic responsibility, stars, God, illiteracy, ambition, divisiveness, survival, Satan, democracy, old friends, mothers and fathers, cities, small towns, cruelty, soccer, intolerance, impulsiveness, love, language, nightlife, freedom, writing, indecision, non-governmental agencies, learning, sex and super powers, and often humorously.

Writing in Tigrinya, Reesom Haile joins a growing movement of African authors who are writing in their own African languages. This rise of African vernaculars, paralleling the rise of truly

independent and democratic African nations, promises a twenty-
first century that will be the African century for literature. For
Reesom Haile, writing in Tigrinya is to go "back to what God has
given you and saying 'I'm not going to give it up.' It's your
freedom...your speech...your self definition...your self expression and
you cannot give it up." With thousands of African languages dating
back—orally and in written form—over the course of millennia, an
unimaginably rich resource is about to be tapped by African writers
and for Africans themselves, yet to be globally shared.

As for my English versions of Reesom Haile's poems, they are
basically the products of an email collaboration between the author
and me, though we have met, become friends and both share expe-
rience in each other's native places and cultures. Most generously,
he would email me a poem's literal translation and I would return it
to him in the form of an English poem based on his original
translation's sense and its appearance in Tigrinya in *Waza ms Qum
Neger nTensae Hager*, the book in which most of the poems had
already been published. In my work, I also took into account how
the poems sounded on an audiocassette of Reesom Haile reciting
his lines. When necessary, he would graciously send back addi-
tional literal versions of his lines to indicate what my English was
still missing, and thus together we'd try again to *join*—which is the
Tigrinya concept for the act of poetry, different from the European
identification of poetry with the process of *making*—our two lan-
guages in the common effort of poetry. Of course, I can only repro-
duce some of the many levels of meaning and association that a
Reesom Haile poem offers to anyone who hears or reads it in the
Tigrinya original. While he and speakers of Tigrinya and English
know what my English versions continue to miss, my poetic faith is
that more is gained than lost in the translation process.

Moreover, there should be more and more translation of Afri-
can-language poets and writers into other languages precisely so that
the mutual exposure can enrich our cultures, our languages and us
all. Thus far, there has been very little of such translation and we
are the poorer for it. The world needs to hear and know the
Shakespeares and the Bibles of African languages, but their real
names are known only by African language writers, while they also

know these European texts precisely because many of them have been translated into African languages.

Tigrinya is widely regarded as a difficult language, as is Eritrea often thought to be a place that is hard to truly understand. Notwithstanding such truisms, my English versions always attempt to represent the spirit if not always achieving the letter of Reesom Haile's work. That we built *We Have Our Voice* through email is fitting since one of his first and most popular poems, "Dehai" or "Voice," is about his publishing most of his poems—sometimes even two a day—on the popular Eritrean website, *Dehai*.

> Speech online
> Can set you free....
>
> ezm! z-ezm! ezm! z-ezm!
> ebum! b-ebum! ebum! b-ebum!
>
> ...We share the screen
> Like the sun
> And our freedom of speech
> Reads the poetry in thought

Throughout Reesom Haile's poetry there are at least two constants. First, not merely on the screen or the page but in reality, his poetry possesses a comprehensive, prudent, not polarizing, universal, accessible, explicit, tried and true, political sense. Uncommon and, perhaps, even unavailable in most American and European poetries today, it is practically in every one of his poems, as if he "kept [it] in his stomach along with the food ...[he] ate a long time ago," as he has remarked. This is apparent in a poem like "Learning from History," on the waxing and waning of Marx and Lenin's influence,

> ... we all make mistakes.
> The evil is in not being corrected.
> Aren't we known
> By what we do, undo and do again?

There is a strong and prevailing sense of political struggle and ideals that might be considered romantic if they were not so realistic and rooted in the indomitable Eritrean political experience of standing alone and winning a 30-year war for independence. Thus, the poet can address the country's leader:

> You wear our crown of leaves
> As long as we're free
> To say yes without force.
> As in the beginning,
> This covenant sways
> With each other's words,
> Leading to the good
> And holding us together
> Not apart in the storm
> To a stranger's delight.
> This way ? That?
> Around? Between?
> With this crown of leaves
> We meet heart to heart:
> With much to learn, but smart
> Enough to know what hurts.
> We choose you
> To wear our crown of leaves.
> It possesses no magic
> But our history and your name.

A second constant in Reesom Haile's poetry is his music, in Tigrinya, of course, but also in the sense of the translations of his poems into English. I could only try to reproduce this sense and not the Tigrinya sound in English, which has its own music. Great poetry, however, should always carry with it, in its original language or translation, a universal music. It is our inheritance and poetry's source, as Reesom Haile also attests in reflecting on his own poetic beginnings:

> It starts with z-ezm! ebum! b-ebum!—which is our drum, our expression of happiness. That is all the struggle is about: that finally we can be happy. I start when I go back to the sound of z-ezm! ebum!—to the . . . everyday songs. . . . then the words start flowing in.

—Charles Cantalupo

ደሃይና አሎና
ምሩጽ ግጥምታት ርእሶም ሃይለ

WE HAVE OUR VOICE

Selected Poems of Reesom Haile

Your Sister

Daughter sister
Your own sweet daughter
Your mother's
Daughter
Her sister's and brother's
Daughter
Your father's daughter
His brother's and sister's
Daughter
Your brother's and sister's
Daughter
Your older brother's
Daughter
Your older sister's
Daughter
Whoever that may be

Daughter of this town
Daughter of your neighbor
Daughter and sister
Of our nation
Your sister
Your daughter
Your grandmother and mother
Your fiancée and your wife
Every daughter
Part of you
Your own sweet daughter
Sister to sister to sister

Respect their rights

ሓብትኻ

ንል አደኻ
ንል አቦኻ
ንል ሓትነኻ
ንል ሓወቦኻ
ንል አሞኻ
ንል አኮኻ
ንል ሓውኻ
ንል ሓብትኻ
ንል ኣያኻ
ንል ሳንዳኻ
ንል መን ኢያ እዚኣ በዃኻ?
ንል ገዛውትኻ
ንል ዓድኻ
ሓብትኻ
ዋላ አደ ዓባይካ ዋላ አደኻ
ዋላ ሕጽይትኻ ዋላ ሰበይትኻ
ዋላ ንልካ መዓረኻ
ኩለን ቆምናኻ ሳላ ባህልኻ
እሞ መሰለን'ዶ ትሕሉወለን ኢኻ?

"*Ova, Signora*"

When the Italians occupied Asmara
We saved a few chickens
In the old district four.
They got fat on the cheap barley,
So we weren't totally poor.
We sold their eggs
White as fine plaster:
"Ova, Signora. Ova, Signora,"
Till our throats were sore.
Thanks to those chickens we survived
While General Baldisera, fortified for war,
Ate omelets.

ኦሻ ሲጮራ

ደረውህ ኔረናና
አብ ኣርባዕተ ኣስመራ
ውሑዳት ተረፍ ኣሞራ
ስገም በሊዐን ዝሃጠራ
ብዓቕመን ጸሕቲረን ሰብ ዝሰተራ
እንቋዕቄሓአን ዝመስል ኖራ
ኦሻ ንሲጮራ ንዓና ባጠራ
ሳላ ደርሁና ዝዓበና
ኦሻ ሲጮራ እናበልና ላሕቲትና
ጀነራል ባልዲሰራ እንታይ'ዶ ጌሩልና?

Foreign Aid

Beg.
I give.
Beg!
I give some more!
So why insult me for giving?

You make me beg.

መን ንመን

ለማኒ !
ተኺቢ !
ለማኒ !
ተኺቢ !
ንተኺቢ ኽኣ ጽርፈ ጌርካዮ?
ወይለከይ ! ዘይተኺቢ መን ንለማኒ ለማኒ ጌሩዎ?

Knowledge

First the earth, then the plow:
So knowledge comes out of knowledge.
We know, we don't know.
We don't know we know.
We know we don't know.
We think
This looks like that —
This lemon, that orange —
Until we taste the bitter.

ፍልጠት

ንሓመድ ድጕሪ የውጽአ
ንፍልጠት ፍልጠት የምጽአ
ነቲ ዘይንፈልጦ ምስ 'ቲ ንፈልጦ
ኣረኣኢና አመሳሲልና
ፈሊጠሃ ሕጅኦስ
እዚ ኽስታይ ኽስታይ ይመስል
ንብል ተቘላጢፍና
በዚ መሰረት . . .
እቲ ለሚን ብርትኹን ይመስለና
ክሳብ ንጥዕሞ ክሳብ ዝመርረና ።

Development

Change.
Like a child, an infant.
"Let's go! Let's go!"
And our household grows.
"Let's run."

We can slow
And sit and stretch
In the sun
Till it sets, but tomorrow
Dawned yesterday.

ምዕባለ

ዓለም ተለዋዋጢት
ከም ፌልዓ
ከም ሕንጢት
ንሳ ትጥል ን'ኺድ ን'ኺድ
ንሕና ሓዳርና ነግፍሕ
ንሳ ትጥል ንጕየ
ንሕና ነሳፍሕ ነሳፍሕ
ንሳ ክትዓርብ ንሕና ንጽበ
ጽባሕ ናብ ትማሊ ክትወግሕ።

Voice

Speech online
Can set you free
It lights my voice
On a screen like the sun

Voice. Voice!
The net sets me free
To think in poetry
The sad will rejoice
The weeping will laugh

In the news like food and drink
In the dark with a candle to think

Sisters, brothers, citizens, drums!
ezm! z-ezm! ezm! z-ezm!
ebum! b-ebum! ebum! b-ebum!
Voice! Voice!

We share the screen
Like the sun
And our freedom of speech
Reads the poetry in thought

ደሃይ

ደሃየ! ደሃየ!
እንኪ ሓሳበይ
ስጥሕለይ ኣብ ጻሓየ።
ደሃየ! ደሃየ!
ኣጻናንዕለይ ዝጉሃየ
ኣብድለይ ዝበኸየ
ዓንግልለይ ዝጠመየ
ኣስትይለይ ዝጸምአየ
ሰላም በልለይ
ንደቂ ዓደየ
ደሃየ! ደሃየ!
ኣብርህለይ ላምባየ
መሬት ምስ መሰየ
እስኪ ኸበሮ
እ-ዝም! ዝም-እዝም! እ-ዝም! ዝም-እዝም!
እ-ቡም! ብ-እቡም! እ-ቡም! ብ-እቡም!
ደሃየ
እንኪ ሓሳበይ
ስጥሕለይ ኣብ ጻሓየ
እንኪ ሓሳበይ
ስጥሕለይ ኣብ ጻሓየ።

Under Consideration

Consider this.
Consider that.
Excellent.
Write it
And propose it
For consideration.

Also consider
The official response,
"It's under consideration."
Who is considering whom?
When? Where?
How? Why?

Give up?
Consider this.

ይሕሰብ ኣሎ

ይሕሰብ ኣሎ
የሕስበኒ ' ሎ
መን ይሕሰብ?
ሓሳባይ
እንታይ ይሕሰብ?
ሓሳብ
መዓስ ይሕሰብ?
ግዜ ሓሳብ
ስለምንታይ ይሕሰብ?
ስለ ሓሳብ
ናይ ብሓቂ ይሕሰብ ኣሎ እምበኣር?
እወ ይሕሰብ ኣሎ።።

Learning from History

We learned from Marx and Lenin:
    To be equal trim your feet
    For one-size-fits-all shoes.
We made their mistakes, too.

    Equally, we all make mistakes.
    The evil is in not being corrected.
        Aren't we known
By what we do, undo and do again?

ማርቆስ-ለኒን

ማርቆስ-ለኒን
ተጋግዮም ኣጋግዮምና
እቲ ሳእንኹም እንተጸበበ
እግርኹም ጓዕምሙ ኢሎሙና
ብሱር ብታሕቲ ክጅምር ማዕርነትና
ዘይጋገ የልቦን
ዘይእረም ጽልኡልና
ካብ ሰብ'ዶ ግብሪ ሰብ ዓብዮና
እቲ ንሰርሓ ንፍንጥሓ ንሰርሓ እንደገና
ንዓና ከም ዝሓሸና
ንሰማማዕ ጥራይ ንሕና።

Sister, Sister

Watch him
Sister, sister
Sharpen the knife

Watch him
Sugar, honey
Take you down

Watch him,
Whatever he's got,
Curse
of God,
Sister, sister

Cruel seed and mad,
Sane and bad

I don't know you, abomination

ሓብተይ ሓብተይ

እብዜ ' ባ እሎ ካ
ሓብተይ ሓብተይ
እንዳበልካስ
ካራ ስሒልካ
ምሕራድ

እብዜ ' ባ እሎ ካ
ሸኮረይ መዓረይ
ገዲፍካስ
ብሓኽለ ምሳር
ምውራድ

ጨኪንካ ንሓብተይ!
ጸሊኡልካ ዝሓወይ!

ጥዑይ ክብለካስ ዓናድ
ስርናይ ክብለካስ ክርዳድ
ንስኽዶ ውላድ፡ መዋረዲ ውራድ!

The Priest

What could Father do?
He begged and begged
Haregu and Gabru
To reconcile,
But they liked to fight instead.
"Haregu and Gabru,
The hell with you,"
Father almost said,
But then he had an idea.
"On holy days they come to church.
Who doesn't like to be seen
Saying prayers and taking Communion?
I'll set a trap and wait."
He met them at the door.
"Haregu, Gabru, I'll make you a deal.
Forgive and forget, or keep out!"
And so they reconciled against their will,
Afraid to be left outside and alone
When everyone they knew was in church:
Exactly what Father knew they would feel.

ኣባት ነፍሲ

ኣባት ነፍሲ እንታይ ይግበሩ
ክልምኑ ውዒሎም ዕርቂ ክገብሩ
ንዒ ተለመኒ ሓረጉ
ንዒ ተለመኒ ጋብሩ
ኣይዕረኾን ኣነ ሓረጉ
ኣይዕረኾን ኣነ ጋብሩ
ዝገበርኩም ግበሩ

ኣባት ነፍሲ ጨነቔዎም
እንታይ ይግበሩ?
ክመጹ እንድየን
ጸለይቲ ክመስላ ቆረብቲ
ናብ ቤተ-ክርስትያን በዓል መዓልቲ
ኣባት ነፍሲ ኣጸዊዶም ጸኒሓመን
ኣብ'ታ ኣፍ ቤተ-ክርስትያን ከቲሮመን
ቂም ሒዝክን ገዛይ ኣይትኣትዋን ኢሎመን
ተዓሪቐን ከይፈተዋ
ፈሪሄን እታ ጽሙዋ
ምስ ሰበን ቤተ-ክርስትያን ክኣትዋ
ንሳ ኢያ ኣባት ነፍሰን ዝደለዮዋ።

21

Desta

Daughter, Desta, born in exile,
Come home for a first time.
Meet your grandmother
Her family, her neighbors —
Your family, your neighbors,
Your country, our home.
Please eat
These vegetables and meat
And a special treat of wild roots.
Or have I spoiled you?

No, Daddy, I love this.
But we need windows.

ደስታ

አብ ስደተይ ወሊደያ
ደስታ ጓለይ ዓደይ ወሲደያ
ምስ ዓባያ አፋሊጠያ
እነውለ ህዝብኺ! እነውለ አዝማድኺ!
እንሆለ ዓድኺ ኢለያ!
ከቀባጥር በብዓይነቱ
ናይ ጾም ናይ ስዕረት አብሊጌያ
ከይትጠምየኒ ንጠዓሟታ
ሽንጦ ኹዕንቲ ወሲኺያ
ኢላትኒ . . . አቦይ መዓረይ ፈትየዮ ኹሉ
እቲ ህድሞና መስኮት ግበረሉ።

The Camel

I'd quit the seminary.
My face looked like a gun.
"What troubles you, my son?
What's all this gloom?"
A priest had come to my room.
"Persevere. Persevere."
"Dear Father," I said, "Enough good cheer.
Look at my country. Why is it
So poor? No place is worse.
What sins did we commit?"
"Easy, my son," he answered.
"Poverty is not a curse.
Think of Jesus' words:
A camel will pass through a needle's eye
Before a rich man will enter heaven."
"Dear Father," I said again,
"Don't you see?
The Lord should let us be rich and die.
We would set a good example
For the camel, our national symbol."

ገመል

አቦይ ቀሺ መጺአም ከበጽሐኒ
ሓዚኑ ሰሚያም ይመስለኒ
መጺአም አጆኻ ክብሉኒ
እንታይ ደአ አሕዚኑካ
ገጽካ አፋሕሺዮካ
ጽንዓት ይሃብካ ኢሎመሙኒ።
ዘሕዘነንስ ናይ ዓደይ ከኾታት
እዘን ኩለን ዓድታት
ክብልወን ሃብታማት
ዓደይ'ዶ ትብሃል ዓዲ ድኻታት
ናይ እንዳመን ሓጥያት?
አጆኻ እዝስ ቀሊል'ዩ ቀሊል
ጐይታና አብ ወንጌል እንታይ ይብል?
ሃብታም ካብ ዝጸድቕ
ገመል ብዓይኒ መርፍእ ክትሓልፍ ይቐልል።
እንቱም አቦና
ዘየህብትመና ግዳ እዚ ጐይታና
ሱቕ ኢሉ መመሰሊ ዝገብረና
ገመል እኮ ኢዮ እቲ አርማና።

The Book

"Lick that fire!"
What did Mother Miniya's little son do?
"I'll drown you in holy water!"
But she was doomed, she knew,
Unless the demon could be stopped.
She wanted her son to learn
And sent him to school.
But when she found the little rascal
Glued with wide eyes
To a book big as a field
She didn't ask or care why.
She knew she'd been a fool.
"Do you want to send me to hell?!"

ዓቢ መጽሓፍ

አደይ ምኒያ
ነቲ ወዳ ሓዊ አልሒሳቶ
ቀጺዓቶ ወጺዓቶ
ከይቅዘፍ ንጸበል ወሲዓቶ
እንታይ ጌሩ?
አምሂራቶ
ክንዲ ገለ ዝኸውን መጽሓፍ
ከንብብ ረኺባቶ
ሰንቢዳ!
ንሱ ንእሽቶ ክንዲ ኸርዳድ
እቲ መጽሓፍ ሰፊሕ ክንዲ ህዳድ
ጠልቃፍ ኮይኑ 'ምበር
እንታይ ኢሉ ዝኸፍቶ
መዓት ከምጽአለይ ከቶ።

Your Head

From birth you need
A door in your head to live.
Mother, father, teacher, preacher,
Sister, brother, relations, friends
Or others of your kind
May have the key
Or it may be lost.
But they still have other ways
To open the lock.
Rancid butter rubbed on your skull
May let the sunshine in.
The phrase, "What are you,
Stupid? dumb?" might throw the bolt.
A flywhisk works on the less fragile.
A wooden spoon, a ruler or a good stick
Does the trick on harder nuts and...
Voila! An open mind!

ርእሰኻ

ክትውለድ ከሎኻ
እቲ ርእሰኻ
ማዕጾ አለዋ
መፍትሒኡ
ምስ አደኻ ምስ አቦኻ
ምስ መምህርካ ምስ ቀሺኻ
ምስ ቤተ-ሰብካ ኮታ ይጸንሕ
እቲ መፍትሕ እንተ ጠፊእዎም
ካልእ ጥበብ አለዎም ወይሉኻ።
መጀመሪያ ልኻይ ይለኽዩኻ
እንተ አበዮም
ዓዋን ዓሻ ደንቆሮ ይብሉኻ
ብመኽሰ ብመንቀርቀር ብጭራ ብመስመር
ቀስ ኢሉ'ም ከይስበሮም ደጋጊሞም
የንኪሕኩሑ ይኹርኩሙኻ አብ ርእሰኻ
ፈላጥ ክፉት ርእሱ ን'ክብሉኻ ምስ ዓበኻ።

The Next Generation

Well traveled and knowing many languages,
The next generation arrives.
Let's rise to the occasion.
"Welcome, Vielkomen, Bien Venue, Ben Venuto!
Let's bathe your tired feet with hot water
And serve the best *injera*,* vegetables, meat and drink.
Take this warm, white *gabi*† to wrap yourself in.
Let's walk the mountains and valleys.
Given to us, we give them to you —
History and culture to read,
A legacy to satisfy your needs
And to share, even with strangers —
On one condition:
Don't give it all away."

* *injera:*   traditional bread.
† *gabi:*   traditional blanket/cloak.

ዝመጽእ ወለዶ

እቲ ዝመጽእ ወለዶ መጺኡ'ሎ
ተንስኡ ብዓጀብ ንቀበሎ
ሃየ በቲ ዝርድእ ዝፈልጦ
መርሓባ! ብደሓን ምጻእ!
ዌልካም! ቢልኮመን!
ብየንቬኑ! በንሸኑቶ! ንበሎ
ሓቦ ንግበር ሓቦ
ማይ አውዒና እግሩ ንሕጸቦ
ነብልዓዮ ነስትዮ ነጽግቦ
ነማሙቐ ጋቢ ንደርቦ
ነሰንዮ ነኽብቦ

በቲ ሩባ በቲ ጎቦ
ምስ ዓበየ ክዓጅቦ
ይመሃር የጽንዓዮ የንብቦ
እቲ ባህሊ እቲ ታሪኽ ዓደቦ።
ሓደራኻ ንበሎ ንላቦ
ሓደራኻ አሕሊፍካ ከይትህቦ
ንሕላፍ መገዲ ንወደ'ቦ።

Show Me the Money

Our people leave us
For fistfuls of dollars.
Arabia, America, Italy, Denmark —
Pots of money —
White Canada, England, Germany —
More pots of money.
The money trail leads all the way
To Australia: anywhere but home.
Who can blame them?
"Get me out of here. Get me a visa.
I'll call my brother. I'll call my sister.
I'll play the lottery. I'll pay the devil."

Our people leave us.
Who can stop the Red Sea
From swallowing them?
The government?
"Pots of money, pots of money."
It even resounds with our parents,
Adding their blessings and dreams
Of a better life for their children:
Fistfuls of dollars for weddings, new houses,
Big funerals and fitting memorials.
"Show us the oil, the gold,
The jobs and pots of money."

Our people leave us.
They have to get in on the take.
They want to bring it home.
But how much more must they give?

ዶላር ብሰንኬሎ

ህዝብና ይወጽእ አሎ
ዶላር ያኢ ከምጽእ ብሰንኬሎ፡፡
ዓዲ ዓረብ አሜሪካ
ዓዲ ጣልያን ዳኒማርካ
ዓዲ ጸዕዳ ካናዳ
ዓዲ እንግሊዝ ጀርመኒ
አውስትራልያ ዓዲ ጅኒ
ካብ'ዛ ዓዲ ጥራይ አውጽአኒ ይብል አሎ

ቪዛ ካብ ሓዉ ዝጽበ'ሎ
ቪዛ ካብ ሓቡቲ ዝጽበ'ሎ
ቪዛ ብሎተሪያ ዝበጽሓ'ሎ
ቪዛ ዝገዝእ አሎ ካብ ደላሎ
ወርቂ'ዲኡ ሸይጡ ዝኸፈሎ
ገሊኦስ ቀይሕ-ባሕሪ ዝወሓጠ'ሎ
ዶላር ያኢ ከምጽእ ብሰንኬሎ

እቲ መንግስቲ እንታይ ይበሎ
አቡኡ አዲኡ ኪድ እናበሎ
ኪድ ዝወደይ ይከአሎ
እዚ ናብራና አቃልሎ
ጽባሕ ገዛ ምስራሕ አሎ
ጽባሕ መርዓ ደርዓ'ሎ
ንቾብሪ ንተዝካር ዝኸፈል አሎ
ኪድ አምጽእ ዶላር ብሰንኬሎ

አበይ አሎ እቲ ዘይቲ አበይ አሎ
አበይ አሎ እቲ ወርቂ አበይ አሎ
አበይ አሎ እቲ ስራሕ አበይ አሎ
ህዝብና በዚሕም ሃባ ዝብሎ
ህዝብና ይደሊ'ሎ እንኻ ዝብሎ
ዶላር ብሰንኬሎ፡፡

The Braggart

I won't gather dust.
So most people like to say.
Son of sea kings,
I take on all comers
Or shoot out their eyes.
One day back when —
Times were tough but who cared? —
I'm taking a stroll around dusk
And suddenly meet
A lion resting by the well.
"Get the fuck up you lazy shit!
Go fart somewhere else!"
I barely shake my stick
And he runs off like a pussy.
I know my lions
And take no prisoners.

አባ ቶጎጋ

እንሆልካ ደአሲ
ወዲ ባሕረ'ጋሲ
ኣነ'ዶ ንርእሰይ ወዳሲ
ድሕር ዘይብል ካብዛ ቃልሲ
ጨማቲ ተኳሲ!
ሓደ መዓልቲ
ከም'ዚ ሎሚ ከይኮነሲ
ኣብ'ታ ማይ ዓዲ ራእሲ
ዕርብርብ ክትብል ምሲይ
ደበኽ እንተበልኩሲ . . .
ኣንበሳ!
ንዓ በል ኣታ ኾላሲ
ኣንታ ፈርሲ
ኣንታ ሓርኢ ኣንታ ፈሲ
ንዓ በል ሕጁሲ . . .
በዛ በትረይ ትንዕ እንተበልኩዋ'ሲ . . .
ጭልጥ ኣውጽእኒ ነፍሲ
ባዕለይ እፈልጥ እሱ'ሲ
ኣንበሳ ኢዩ ነይሩ ኣንበሳ'ሲ
ፈሊጡኒ ደኣ ከም ዘየናሕሲ!

A Cross

A cross a cross
We welcome the cross
One more cross
To cross our loss, inside and out
Crosses galore to sing without doubt
Unaware, poor, we wear the cross
A cross a cross a cross
We welcome the cross
But need more crosses
To hang our losses

መስቀል

መስቀለ መስቀለ! ሆ!
ድሓን ተቓልቀለ! ሆ!
መስቀል ከም ዘይብልና
መስቀል ነጋይሽ ንሕና
ኣብ ሃገርና ህዝብና ሰብና
ጸር ኣብ ርእሲ ጸርና
ተደሪዉ ዘሎ
ናይ ድኽነት መሃይምነት መንጠሊና
ኣበይ? መዓስ? ክንሰ'ቝሎ ኢና . . .
መስቀሊ 'ምበር
መስቀልስ ኣሎና
መሊኡ!

The Leader

You wear our crown of leaves
As long as we're free
To say yes without force.
As in the beginning,
This covenant sways
With each other's words,
Leading to the good
And holding us together
Not apart in the storm
To a stranger's delight.
This way ? That?
Around? Between?
With this crown of leaves
We meet heart to heart:
With much to learn, but smart
Enough to know what hurts.
We choose you
To wear our crown of leaves.
It possesses no magic
But our history and your name.

ሕራይ ኣብለና

ሕራይ ኣብለና ብዓል ቆጽሊ
ብሓይሊ ዘይኮነስ
ብዋዕላ ብባይቶ ብዕሊ ብጥሊ
ከም ቀደምና
ንበሃሃል ንሕና ንሕና
ንፋስ ኣይነእቱ ኣብ መንጎና
ከይንኽውን መፍቶ ወደ'ቦና
ከምዚ'ዶ ሓይሽ ከምዚ
ከምቲ'ዶ ሓይሽ ከምቲ
ልብኻ ሃበና እንካ ልብና
ለባማት ኢና እንተዘይተመሃርና
ዘሕምመናስ ንፈልጠ ባዕልና
ከም ቀደምና ከይንኽይድ ኣብ ጠቢብና
ኣቃዪሕና ናባኻ ኣቃዪሕና
ሽም ኣሎካ ኣብቲ ታሪኽና።

If I Had...

If I had a book
If I had a teacher
If I had a school
If I had an education
If I had a job
If I had a hammer
If I had a house
If I had money
If I had a man
If I had a woman
If I had a child

If I had....

መጽሐፍ እንተዝህሉስ

መጽሐፍ እንተዝህሉስ
መምህር እንተዝህሉስ
ቤት-ትምህርቲ እንተዝህሉስ
ትምህርቲ እንተዝህሉስ
ስራሕ እንተዝህሉስ
ገንዘብ እንተዝህሉስ
ገዛ እንተዝህሉስ
ሰብኣይ እንተዝህሉስ
ሰበይቲ እንተትህሉስ
ቆልዓ እንተዝህሉስ
ቆልዓ እንተትህሉስ
መጽሐፍ እንተዝህሉስ።

Speak Out

To speak out and to be spoken about,
Or to see no evil, hear no evil,
Shut up, keep it to yourself
And only complain in private?
That is *not* the question.
Read the constitution
Of our democratic state.
Exercise your rights
To tell it like it is,
Write as you see fit
And get a good night's sleep.
You also have the right to take
Back what you say by mistake.
The freedom to express
Cannot be given up.
It comes from God.
Be free and brave.
Only one prison remains:
Our minds.

ከይብሉና

ከይብሉና ንብል ከይብሉና
ሰሚዕና ከም ዘይሰማዕና
ርኢና ከም ዘይረኣና
ክንነብር ኣፍና ዓጺና
ደሓር ክንሓምዮም ተሓቢእና
ኣንቢብኩሞ ዲኹም እቲ ቅዋምና
ሰሚዕኩሞ ዲኹም እቲ መንግስትና
ናጻ እኮ ኢና መሰል ኣሎና
ዝመሰለና ተዛሪብና
ዝመሰለና ጽሒፍና
ክንሓድር ገዛና
ጌጋ ይኸልኣልና እንተተጋጊና
ደጉሽተተይ ንብል ከም ሰብና
ንሰብ ግን ኣይነረክብን
እግዚሄር ዝሃበና
መን'ከ ደፊሩ ክቐበለና?
መቓኍሕ የልቦን ብዘይካ ርእሰ መቓኍሕና
ኣጆኹም ኣጆኸን ደቂ ዓደይ ናጻ ኢና።

We Have

We have men and women
Who sacrifice their lives.
We have a nation.
We have women and men
To gather and provide.
Men and women who lead.
We have independence.
We have equality and justice
We have women and men.
We have black, white, and red.
We have men and women
Without end in the struggle
To grow, study and persist.
Who think and think again
To teach, learn and know.
We have women and men
Without the lust for power.
Who stand up or down
With our consent.
We have God and a future.
We have men and women
Who belong in our nation
And we belong with them.
Rejoice, I say it again.
We have women and men.
Rejoice.

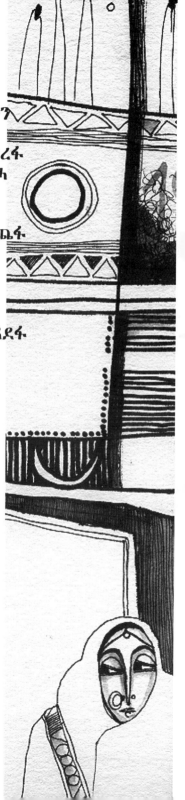

ኣለዉና / ኣለዋና

ንሃገሮም / ንሃገረን ህይወቶም / ህይወተን
ዘሕለፉ / ዘሕለፋ
ንሃገሮም / ንሃገረን ናጽነት ዘትረፉ / ዘትረፋ
ንህዝቦም / ንህዝበን ዘመርሑ / ዘመርሓ
ዝጥርንፉ / ዝጥርንፋ
ኣለዉና / ኣለዋና
ንፍትሕን ንፍርድን ዘወናጨፉ / ዘወናጨፋ
ሌላን ጉሌላን ዝጽይፉ / ዝጽይፋ
ዘይብሉና / ዘይብላና ቀይሑ / ቀይሓ
ሓርፈፉ / ሓርፈፋ
ኣለዉና / ኣለዋና
ንሃገር ከማዕብሉ / ከማዕብላ ዝጸደፉ / ዝጸደፋ
ንመጻኢና ዝሓስቡ / ዝሓስባ
ዝፈላሰፉ / ዝፈላሰፋ
ዝምህሩ / ዝምህራ ዝመሃሩ / ዝመሃራ
ዘንብቡ / ዘንብባ ዝጽሕፉ / ዝጽሕፋ
ኣለዉና / ኣለዋና
ብፍቓድና ዝስለፉ / ዝስለፋ
ብፍቓድና ዝግለፉ / ዝግለፋ
ንስልጣን ዘይሃርፉ / ዘይሃርፋ
ኣለዉና / ኣለዋና።
ናይ እግዚኄር ንግዚኄር
ናይ ብሔር ንብሔር
ዝገድፉ / ዝገድፋ
ኣለዉና / ኣለዋና
ክሓልፈፈልና እንድዩ ክሓልፈፈልና።

Stars in the Sky

A sky full of stars —
They outnumber us by far,
Yet we have more light.

A night full of stars
Fade in the sun.
But one

Called the shepherds
And three kings to our Lord
And they adored

The light
Like stars, despite
The wintry darkness.

Light can be borrowed,
Light can be bred.
We have more light
Because we're united.

ከዋኽብቲ ሰማይ

ከዋኽብቲ ሰማይ
ካባና ይበዝሑ
ካባና ነይበርሁ

ካብ ጸሓይ ቀዲሓም
ለይቲ ኣውራሕሪሓም
እንታይ'ከ ሰሪሓም

ሓደ ካብኣቶም
ጓሶት መሪሑ
ናብ ጐይታና ኣብጺሑ

ምስ ክንድ'ዚ ብዝሓም
ክንድ'ዚ ቀዲሓም
እቲ ለይቶም ብለይቱ'ሎ

ርእዮና ንሕና
በሪቁ'ሎ ለይትና
ኣይበዛሕና ኣይተለቃሕና
ሓቢርና ጥራይ ሓቢርና።

God Save Us

Not men but the rule of law
Reveals my right to live
Free of fear.
Yet thousands of the same species
Sacrifice their lives
For the same right, too,
With plenty to go around
For all, great or small.

God save us.

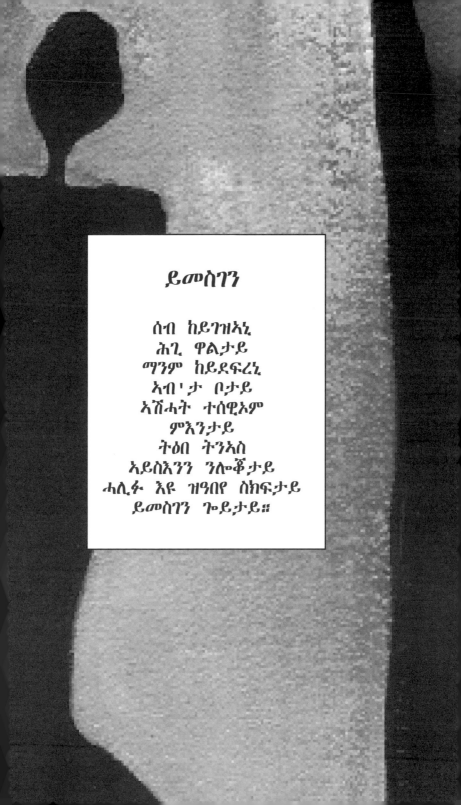

ይመስገን

ሰብ ከይገዝእኒ
ሕጊ ዋልታይ
ማንም ከይደፍረኒ
ኣብ ' ታ ቦታይ
ኣሸሓት ተሰዊኦም
ምእንታይ
ትዕበ ትንኣስ
ኣይስእንን ንሉኞታይ
ሓሊፉ እዩ ዝዓበየ ስክፍታይ
ይመስገን ጐይታይ።።

Satan

What have I done?
No. Satan is the one.
His name
Spells shame.
He knows his place
Below the human race.
I have free will.
But call me "a devil"
And I feel good,
Like I rule the neighborhood.
Prince of hell . . . shit.
Satan is you and me.
Trouble makes three.
We have a bad habit:
Saying, "Satan's to blame."
I coil like a snake
With no peace to make.

ሰይጣን

ሰይጣን እንታይ ጌሩ ወሪዱዎ
ፍጥረቱ ኮይኑዎ!
ወዲ-ሰብ ተዓዘብዎ ብስድሪ ሓሊፉዎ
«ሰይጣን'ዩ ሰይጣን» እንተበልዎ
ክጸወትዎ ክንእድዎ
ሓቂ መሲሉዎ
ግብረ ሰይጣን ለሚዱዎ
ንሳጥናኤል ጸዊዑዎ ኢሉዎ
ኣነ ሰይጣን ንስኻ ሰይጣን
መኒና ይኹን ጉብጣን
ናይ ጸበባን ጣጣን?
ሰይጣን ሰይጣን ኣይትበሉ
ሰብ'ዩ ሰይጣን ብኣመሉ
ከም ተመን ተዓኚሊሉ ዝሕሉ
ኣብዛ ዓለም ሰላም ከይትህሉ።

Democracy

Greek seedling,
Dear democracy,
Please come with me to Africa.
I have water for the heat
And fire for the cold.
My medicine of local holy water
Will control the termites
And keep you rooted.
Forget your fear.
Come live with me.
I need your shade to rule
When the representatives meet,
With only an acacia
To prick me with its thorns.

ደሞክራሲ

ደሞክራሲ
ናይ ኣቴንስ ፈልሲ
ክልምነኪ ሕጂሲ
ንዒንዶ ኣፍሪቃ ተሳገሪ
ሃሩር ዲኺ ጸሊእኪ ቀኒሪ?
ማይ ኣሎኩም ንዳህሪ
ጓህሪ ኣሎኩም ንቖሪ
ኣነ ጸላእኩ ፍልሓ ምልሓ
ኣነ ፈራሕኩ ብሱረይ ከይምሓ።።

ኣሎ'ኹልኪ ኩስኳሲ
ንፍልሓስ ኣሎና ፈውሲ
ጸበል ዓዲ ራእሲ
ንዒ ምሳይ ተበገሲ
ናይ ዓደይ ካብ ኮንኩ ወናኒ
ኣብቲ ባይቶ ጽላል ክትኮንኒ
እቲ ጮዓስ እንዳወግአኒ
እምበር ጮዓስ ኔሩኒ።።

What to Do

Like it or not,
We have a president
And if we had no president
We would invent one.
Astride the president's shoulders,
Monkeys like us look strong,
Call it what you will.
But when will we get off?
The president has work to do.
We have work, too.

እየ ንሕና

ፈቲና ጸሊእና
ኢሳያስ እንተዘይሀሉ
ኢሳያስ ምፈጠርና
ኣብ ክሳዱ ከም ኣህባይ ትሓንጊርና
እቲ ጉልበቱ ጉልበትና ኣስመሲልና
ገሌና ንውድስ ገሌና ንወቅስ ገሌና . . .
ንውረደሉ ደኣ ንኺድ ብኣእጋርና
ግቡኡ ይግበር ግቡእና ነይተርፈና።

Friends

A holy trinity
From the beginning,
Three ants crawling in the mud,
We planted our friendship,
Swearing with swallowed pebbles —
Our hands cupping sacred soil
Of home —
That we would bloom together.
And so we did,
In the same breath,
Two writers and one driver.
We'll always laugh together.
We also cry
When we see, hear and speak
What we remember.

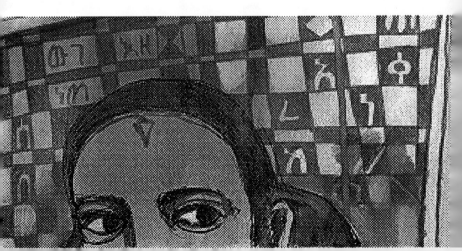

እዕሩኸ

ከም ሰለስተ ስላሴ
ሰለስተ ኢ.ና
እዕሩኸ ኢ.ና
ካብ ቀደም ጀሚርና
ከክንዲ ጸጸ ኸለ.ና
አብቲ ሓመድ ፈፈው እናበልና
ዕርክነት ተኺልና
ዕርክነትና ከጸድቀልና
ምሒልና ጥሒልና
ጸጸር ውሒ.ጥና
ሓመድ ቀ.ሒ.ምና
ጸበል ናይ ዓድና
ተመሲሉ.ልና!
ክሳብ ሕጇ ትኸ ትንፋስ ኢ.ና
አሎ.ና ገና ብዕምርና
ክልተ ጸሓፍቲ ሓደ ዘዋር መኪ.ና
ንርኢ ንሰምዕ ንዛረብ አሎ.ና
ሓንሳእ ንስሕቅ ሓንሳእ ንበኪ ዘዘኪ.ርና።

Mothers Like Mine

You knew what lay ahead.
"May the Lord take me before you,"
You often said
To all the sons and daughters
You've had to bury.
We didn't listen.
But your sacrifice
Has given birth:
Behold Eritrea,
Fruit of thy womb.

በዓል ኣደይ

ዝፈለጥክን ፈሊጥክን
ክሕሽክን ንዓታትክን
ቅድሜኻ ይግበረኒ
ቅድሜኺ ይግበረኒ
ትብላና ኔርክን

መን ሰሚዑክን
ክንደይ ዘይወለድክን
ክንደይ ዘይቀበርክን ብደውክን

ጽንዓት ይሃብክን
ንኸንቱ ኣይኮነን መስዋእትኽን
ሃገርም ኣምሊሶማ ጀጋኑ ደቅኽን
እንጌለት ኤርትራ ፍረ ከርስኽን።

Thy Brother's Envy

Lord, you've never granted me a wish.
Now, please, just one.

Never? OK. But only one,
And call your brother.
I'll give him twice as much.

What? Double what I get?
Then I beg you
Blind me in one eye.

ሕሱም ቅንኢ

አንታ እግዚሄር ተለመን ክልምነካ
ጸዲ ቅካለይ ዘይትፈልጥ ጸዲ ቅካ
ሓንሳእ ት ኹ በለይ ንማሕላ ክ ኹ ነካ

ካብ በልካ . . .
ንገረኒ እቲ እትደልዮ
ነቲ ሓ ው ኽ ጸ ው ዓዮ
ንዓኻ ሂብ ንዕኡ ዕጽፈ ክፈ ድዮ

ወይለከይ !
አነ ለሚ ነስ ዕጽፈ ንሓወይ
ከም ኡ እ ን ተ ኹ ይ ኑ ስ ወደይ
ሓ ን ቲ ዓይነይ አ ን ቀ ረ ለይ ።

In the City

City snakes have no eyes
But wind themselves around you
Like wet leather.
When it dries
Their teeth are the surprise.
City snakes rule
By keeping what they have.
They take what you have, too.

ኣብ ከተማ

ኣብ ከተማ
ኣሎዉ ኣትማን
ዓይኒ ዘይብሎም
ጥራይ ኣስናን
የዘንግዑኻ
ይቕኑቴኻ
ከም ምራን ከም መጽዓን
ሓንቲ ሕጊ ኣላቶም
እታ ናቶም ናቶም
ናቶም እታ ናትካ ከማን።

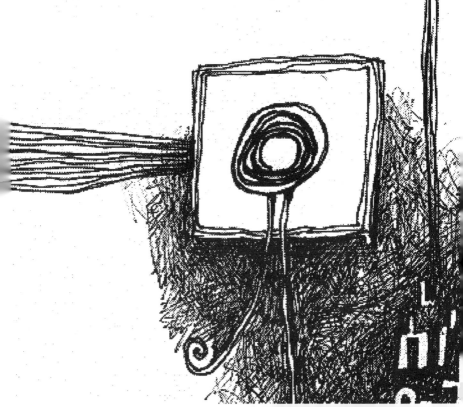

Dog's Tail

"I dance better,"
Said the tail to its dog,
"Let's fight!"
Too tired, the dog
Bit it off,
Spit it in the dust
And left,
Growling, "Behave."

ጭራ ኸልቢ

ጭራ ኸልቢ ምስ ከልቢ ተባኢሳ
ኣነ እስዕስዕ ኣነ እቐኈጸ ክትብል ንሳ
ከልቢ ሆየ ረብሪብዋ
ካብ ጉንዳ በንቄሳ
ገዲፎዋ ከዶ ኣብ ሓመድ ፈሲሳ
ጠባይ ግዳ ዘይትገብር ንሳ?

Soccer Ball

How do you do it?
Always so pumped and proud
And the darling of the crowd
While you're endlessly slapped around,
Beat against the wall,
Chased, caught, trapped,
Kicked, butted, kneed,
Bounced and called out of bounds
For simply desiring the goal
And, perhaps, a kiss.
I admire you, but please
Accept my sympathies.

Shut up, you fool.
Who do you think you are?
What can you really know about me?
You're like a ball that's never touched a field.
Your only game is money.
You want a life like mine?
You'll need the rules
And a good referee.

ኩዕሶ

ኣንቲ ኩዕሶ እንታይ ኢዩ ምስጢርኪ
ኩሉ ግዜ ምስ ኩራዕኪ
ኮረር መረር ትብሊ ልብኺ ነፊሕኪ
ኣይውሓደን ዝጸፍዓኪ ዘላግዓኪ
ብእግሩ ብኢዱ ብቴስታ ብበርኩ
ዘንጥረኪ ጠረብረብ ዘብለኪ
ዝጎየኪ ሓሊፉ ዝኸትረኪ
ሓንሳእ ፎሪ የውጽኣኪ
ሓንሳእ ጎል የእትወኪ
ይዋእ ሓብተይ እንታይክ ረኺብኪ?
ናብራ ኩዕሶ እንታይ ኣፍሊጡካ
ማይ ኣይጥዓመን ሓድሽ'የ ሓንጒልካ
እንተ ትሸጦስ ገንዘብ መውጸኣልካ
ከምዚ ናተይ ንዓኻ ይፍጠረልካ
እንተዘይኣመንካ ሕተቶ ኣልቢትሮ እንሆልካ
መን ኣሎ ንዓይ ዝቐልዐ
ሕገይ ከየኸበረ ከይመልአ?

The Tongue

God started with the tongue.
It plotted with your lips, palate
And teeth to get your lungs
To breathe more than CO_2 and oxygen:
Words
And a language to create
Who you are
And what communities share.
Similarly sharp,
Your eyes advised your head,
Hands and heart how to invent
Letters
To save words from certain death
If they only remained in the air.
If you have a problem with any name,
Get to the root of it:
The tongue's to blame.
Thus the ancient wisdom in being told
Hold your tongue.

መልሓስ

መልሓስ ህያብ እግዚኣብሔር
ምስ ትንሓግ ምስ ኣስናን ምስ ከናፍር
ምስ ሳንቡእ ምስ ጎሮሮ ተሻሪኻ
ፈጠረት ይብሃል ቋንቋኻ መለለዩኻ
መተሓባበሪ ምስ ህዝብኻ
ኣብቲ ዓለማኦም ኣብቲ ዓላማኻ
ኣዕይንቲ ተዓዚበን
ምስ ልቢ ምስ ሓንጎል ምስ ኣእዳው
ተማኺረን
እዛ መልሓስ ትብሎ ኣብ መጽሓፍ ነስፍሮ
ተባሃሂለን
ጀመራ ክዓቕርኦ ፈደላት ፈጢረን
ይኹን እምበር
ብሰበብ ቋንቋ
ዝመጸካ ኣምርሮ
መልሓስ'ያ ትጾር
መልሓስኩም ሓዙ ይበሃል
ካብ ቀደም ጀሚሩ ካብ ዱሮ።

Truth

We won't call *true*
Anything less
Than what three witnesses
Swear on their lives
To have seen or heard
With their own eyes or ears
And independently agree to.
We have no other defense.
Win or lose, it's a struggle,
And sometimes we need to use
The Bible as a crutch.

ሓቅነት

ሰለስተ ሰባት
ኣብአ ኔሮም
ብእዝኖም ሰሚያም
ብዓይኖም ርእዮም ኣተከኑሮም
ምሒሉ̈ም ክብሉ ን̈ዕምሮም
እንተ መስኪሮም
ሓቂ ን̈ብል
ሓቅነት ማሕበራዊት
ብዘይካ ዝነበረ ዝሰምዐ ዝረኣየ
የብላ̈ን ሰራዊት
ሓንሳእ ትስዓር ሓንሳእ ትስዕር
ተመርኮሳ ዳዊት።።

Our Language

Welcome
To our language.
Taste
The sauce
With spicy melted
Butter,
Berbere pepper
And sea salt.
The bones are big
Not only for the flavor.
But take them
Like communion.

ቒንቒና

እዚ ቛንቒና
እዚ ትግርኛ
ክጥዕም
ጨው አሎዎ!
ክልምልም
ጠስሚ'ሎዎ!
ክቖምም
በርበረ'ሎዎ!
ክፍግም
ዓጽሚ'ሎዎ!
ቅረብዎ ቀረብዎ
አስተማቕርዎ።

Tigrinya

Nobody genuflects
To our language.
It's straight
From the heart
And simply understood
To resurrect
The nation.
"Hail Mary, Help us, Hail Mary,"
We sing like scythes.

ትግርኛ

እቲ ጀንቋና
ክንብለሉ እምበር
መዓስ ክንስግደሉ
ኢ.ልና ' ኸ
ተሰማሚዕና
ተሓባቢርና
ዓድና ከነጣጥሓሉ
ሆይ ማሪያም ሓግዝና!
ሆይ ማሪያም ሓግዝና!
ሆይ ማሪያም ሓግዝና!

Asmara By Night

After work I like to stop
At Rita's Bar Gurgusum.
The fighters who won the war drink there.
"My heroes! Good evening."
The men greet me back.
But where are the women who fought?

"Ciao, Rita." "Amore!"
"Please help me out.
A White Horse or a cold one
With the old-style Melotti cap?"
"Amore! Do what you like. Don't ask me.
Peace. It's a free country."

አስመራ ብለይቲ

ስራሕ ውዒለ ምስ መሰየ
እንዳ በዓል ሪታ
ባር ጉርጉሱም ድዩ'ታ?
ተኣልየ
ድሓን'ዶ ኣምሲኹም ተጋደልቲ
ድሓን'ዶ ኣምሲኽን . . . ወይለይ
ኣበይ ድአ ኸይደን እተን ኣንስቲ ተጋደልቲ?
ሪታ . . .
ቻው ኣሞረ!
እንታይ ክሰቲ
ዋይት ሆርስ'ዶ ክሰቲ
ወይስ ቢራ ነበር ናይ መሎሙቲ?
ሓንቲ? ዝሕልቲ?
ኣሞረ!
ከም ጁባኻ ግበርየ!
ከም ድላይካ ንበርየ!
ሰላምያ ሃገርየ!

My Freedom

By the flesh of my martyrs
Freedom is mine
Forever

Take my eyes and ears
All my senses
Freedom forever

Take my hands and feet
Take my limbs
Freedom is mine

By the flesh of my martyrs
Take my bones, blood
And all this life

I am freedom
Forever
By the flesh of my martyrs

ናጽነተይ

ናጽነተይ
ስጋ ስዉእተይ
ዘልኣለም ናተይ

እንኩ ኢደይ
እንኩ እግረይ
መሓውርተይ

እንኩ ዓይነይ
እንኩ እዝነይ
ህዋሳተይ

እንኩ ስጋይ
እንኩ ዓጽመይ
ህይወተይ

ናጽነተይ
ስጋ ስዉእተይ
ዘልኣለም ናተይ

It Is Written

You can't read
But you like to say "it is written,"
Meaning, "Doomed.
Our bad luck again. We've sinned."
But think. Imagine.
What if God gives you life
To make it what you will?
You can't refuse
Or hide behind your mother's apron.
No excuses.
Because you're a human being
Not a stone
You can choose:
Make or break.
God gives you life,
But it's one visit per person.
At the end, when you are asked,
    "What have you done?"
Speak up and keep moving.
A new line forms on the right.

ጽሑፍና

ጽሑፍና ትብሉ ከም'ተንብቡ
ዕድልና'ዩ ትብሉ እንተጸቢቡ
ሓጥያትና'ዩ ተደሪቡ ተደራሪቡ
ንዑ ድአ ተጣበቡ
እግዚኄርሲ ሂቡ ኢዩ ሂቡ
ህይወትኩም ባዕልኹም ክትናብዩ
ምረጽ አይትበሉኒ
መሪጽኩም ሃቡኒ
ምኽንያት ክኹኑኒ
ቅናት አደይ ሓንኮሉኒ
አይንሰብን ንእምኒ
ህይወትኩም ናትኩም ንሓላልኩም
ወይ አልሚዕኩም ወይ አጥሬእኩም
ክሓተኩም'ዩ ክሓተኩም
ህይወት ዝሃበኩም
እንታይ ጌርኩም ከመይ ጌርኩም?
ቃል-ዓለም ግደፉ
ንዑ ተበገሱ ተሰለፉ
በዛ ዓለም ሓንሳብ ኢኹም ትሓልፉ
አብ'ዛ ዓለም በይንኹም ነይትተርፉ።

The Rule

Justice or mercy?
Human or divine?
Will or law?
Fate or choice?
Desire or command?
Yours or mine?
Woman or Man?
God or child?
Love or fear?
Conscience or conquest?
Father or mother?
Brother or sister?
Always or sometimes?

ሰብዶ እግዚኄር?

አቲም አሕዋትና
ሰብ'ዶ እግዚኄር
ይግዝእና?
እግዚኄር ብፍቓዱ
ሰብ ብፍቓድና
እግዚኄር ብድላዩ
ሰብ ብድላይና
እግዚኄር ፈትዩ
ሰብ ፈቲና
እግዚኄር መሪጹ
ሰብ መሪጽና
እግዚኄር ብሕልና
ሰብ ብሕግና
እግዚኄር ራሕሪሑ
ሰብ ፈሪዱ ፈቲሑ
እግዚኄር ከም አቦና/አዴና
ሰብ ከም ሓውና/ሓብትና
እግዚኄር ንዘልዓለምና
ሰብ እንዳ'በራረና።

Jerusalem

Are you the famous one,
David's own and the daughter of Solomon?
Jerusalem?
Or are you a wild animal,
Gold draping your head,
Piercing your nose
And flowing down your neck and breasts?
Many call you beautiful.
"You belong to me," claims the Jew.
"Let me share you," the Muslim offers.
"Come to me," the Christian commands.
Do you have magic between your thighs?
Not enough for Jesus, Mary or Mohammed.
They ascended, taking their bodies with them
And leaving you behind.
I know someone, too, with more affections:
Asmara. My steady who always provides.
May God protect her and me from your charms.

ኢየሩሳሌም

ንስኺ 'ዲ ኺ ኢየሩሳሌም ዝብሉኺ
ጓል ሰሎሞን ጓል ዳዊት ዝብሉኺ
ኣነ ጓለይ ጓል ኣራዊት ምበልኩኺ

ተሸሊምኪ ...
ወርቂ ኣብ ርእስኺ ወርቂ ኣብ ክሳድኪ
ወርቂ ኣብ ኣፍንጫኺ ወርቂ ኣብ ኣፍ ልብኺ
ብሪቕሪቕ ውሪቕሪቕ ኢልኪ 'ምበር ካብ መን
ትጽብቒ ንስኺ?

እፈልጥ 'የ
ብዙሓት 'ዮም ንጓይ! ንጓይ! ዝብሉኺ
እቶም ኣይሁድ ይደልዩኺ ክብሕቱኺ
እቶም እስላም ይደልዩኺ ክመቕሉኺ
እቶም ክርስትያን ይደልዩኺ ክስብኩኺ
እታ ሰልፍኪ እንታይ ቀቢርክላ ኢኺ?

እፈልጥ 'የ
ብስግኣም ብንፍሶም ዝሃደሙ ካባኺ
በዓል ክርስቶስ በዓል መሓመድ ዓሪጎም ሓዲጎምኺ
ማርያምስ ኣይፈለሰትን 'ዶ ብዘይካኺ

ክሊ በዓኺ . . .
ኣነ ኣይቀንእን ብኣኺ
ኣለዋና በረኸቲ ብባህሪኤን ብመልክዐን ዝበልጻኺ
ሰጦ ምስ በላ ሓንብ–መንብ ዘይብለን ከማኺ
በዓል ኣስመራ እንታይ ከተውጽእለን ደሊኺ
ኪዲ ድኣ ኣይልከየልና ሕብርኺ።

NGOs

Don't pray for the NGOs.
They come and go,
Eating half of what they give
And wasting the leftovers
Supposed to be for us.
Yet only our pain gets them business
And praise, networking their own
Governments and press.
They say we're in good hands
But our cotton sets the beer
In their palm, leaving the other hand free
To perform our work of survival,
As if they must borrow our watch
To tell us the time
While they will never go hungry.
But why show them our anger?
So they can get us in more trouble?
Better to help them believe and
Understand we've always been independent
And we can talk about their mistakes.
Maybe a few NGOs
Will even come back and help.

ኤንጀአ

ንኤንጀአ
መን ከይብል እግዚአ
እቲ ዘምጽእአ
ፍርቁ ይበልዕአ
ፍርቁ ይድርብይአ
ተዛሚደን . . .
ብኣፈን ተናኢደን
ብመንግስቲ ዓደን
ብጋዜጣ ዓደን
በቲ ስቓይና ነጊደን
ስዋና ብጡጥና ለሚደን
ኣብቲ ስራሕና ናይ ዘእተዋ ኢደን
መን ከማና ለሚደን
ሰዓት ክነግራና ሰዓትና ወሲደን
ምኽድሲ ይኺዳ ዓደን
ኣይክስእናን ንኸብደን
ኮሪና ኮርፈፍ ኢልና ኣይንስደደን
ነግራማት'የን ኣልየን ከይደን
ንምሃረን ነረድኣየን
ብዘይ ብኣና ብሃልቲ ኢየን
ቀስ ኢልና ጌጋአን ነርድኣየን
ኣይሰእናን ዝምለሳ ክሕግዛ ደልየን።

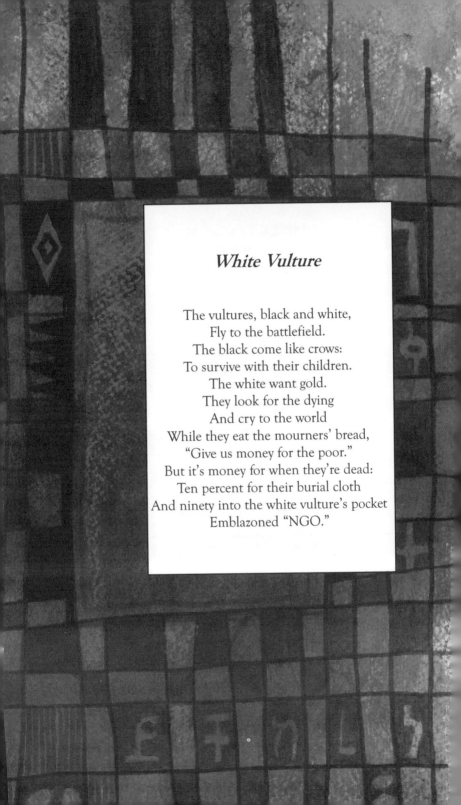

White Vulture

The vultures, black and white,
Fly to the battlefield.
The black come like crows:
To survive with their children.
The white want gold.
They look for the dying
And cry to the world
While they eat the mourners' bread,
"Give us money for the poor."
But it's money for when they're dead:
Ten percent for their burial cloth
And ninety into the white vulture's pocket
Emblazoned "NGO."

ጸዕዳ ኣሞራ

ጸሊም ኣሞራ ንደቁ
ጸዕዳ ኣሞራ ንወርቁ
ይንየዩ 'ሎ፡ወ.
ዓውደ ውግእ ከዘልቁ

ጸሊም ኣሞራ
ኳኽ ብሓበራ
ምእንቲ ናብራ
ጸዕዳ ኣሞራኽ
ከሎኽ ዝይተሃወኽ
ምስ ሞትካ እንዳበኽ
ቂሬጣ እንዳሓየኽ
ገንዘብ ሃቡኒ ምእንቲ ድኽ
ገንዘብ ሃቡኒ ምእንታኽ
ተስዓ ንጅቡኡ ዓሰርተ መግነዚኽ
ጸዕዳ ኣሞራ ኤንጇኦ ኸኣ ይብሉኽ

Our Son, Reesom

As Reesom's father give him good advice.
He might end up in jail.
Why does he waste his time?
A word to the wise is "hold your tongue"
But he continues to rhyme
Like a know-it-all everyday on *Dehai*,*
Encouraged by the chorus, "Go doc go!"
As if they could bail him out tomorrow.

As Reesom's mother you can warn him, too.
What is he, looking for trouble?
All this joining of words and names
And standing in the ranks of poets
Might make him a target,
The enemy of his country:
Just another cultural subversive
Pinning the tail on Tigrinya.

Like father like mother like son:
Except for God, Reesom fears no one.
The jury of his peers,
His friends at school, say
He's added to the culture
And deducted only from his pay.

* *Dehai*: popular Eritrean web site (www.dehai.org)

አቦ ርእሶም

አቦ ርእሶም ንወድኹም ም'ኽሩዎ
ከይአስሩዎ ሓደ መዓልቲ ከይአስሩዎ
እንታይ ገደሰ አፍካ ሓዝ በልዎ
ሎምስ ሓሜን ኮይኑ በጺሑዎ
ባህሊ ማህሊ እንታይ ተሪፉዎ
አብ'ቲ ደሃይ አብ ጽሑፍ አስፈሩዎ
አለዉዎ አጆኻ ዶተር ዝብሉዎ
ጽባሕ ንግሆ ከም ዝወሓሱዎ

አደ ርእሶም ወድ'ኽን ም'ኸራ
መዓት ከይትርእያ መከራ
ግደፍ በልአ አውራ አውራ
እቲ ግጦሚ! እቲ ማሰ! እቲ ፈኽራ!
ከይመስሎዎ ንሃገሩ ዘማረራ
ከይመስሎዎ ንባህሉ ዝደፈራ
ንትግርኛ አውጺኡላ ጭራ

ናይ መን ድአ ክወስድ ናይ አቡኡ
ናይ መን ድአ ክወስድ ናይ አዲኡ
ወድና አይፈርሕን ብዘይካ ፈጣሪኡ
ሕተቱሉ ንመማህርቱ ንመሳቱኡ
አይብሉ'ኹምን ንባህሊ አጥፊኡ
እንተዘይመሊኡ ካብ ጆቡኡ አውጺኡ።

Lete Michael

. . . Daughter of St. Michael,
Cornrows on your head
And thighs to comfort a heart
Like a morsel of bread

It came to me today,
That song I hadn't heard for years
From when the Italians ruled.

Lete Michael, Lete Michael,
Cornrows on your head . . . .

Was she fooled by such praise?
Who was her family?
Lete Michael, Lete Michael
Who brought her shame?

Four churches of St. Michael,
And neither the Orthodox
Nor Catholic, *Of the Hill*
Nor *Of the Plain*
Have a word to add about her.

. . . thighs to comfort my heart
Like a morsel of bread.

Bread? Why not spicy meat,
Injera at least, what an Eritrean likes to eat?
Her lover must have been Italian.

Lete Michael, Lete Michael
I still can't explain the
Cornrows on your head . . . .

If anyone can, please help
For our Holy Mother's sake.

ለተኪኤል

«ለተኪኤልየ ተቔነኒ
ሰለፉ ዝጥዕም ባኒ!»
እዚኣ ካብ ዝሰምዕ ዘበናት ኣሎኒ
ትዝ ኢላህኒ ዘኪረያ ሎሚ
መን'ያ ለተኪኤል ጓል መን'ያ
መን'ዩ ከምዚ'ሉ ዝነኣዳ ዝሓመያ?

ሓቲተላ . . .
ንሚካኤል ተዋህዶ ንሚካኤል ኩተሊኸ
ንሚካኤል ታሕታይ ንሚካኤል ላዕላይ
ኣይንፈልጣን ኢሎሙኒ ናይ እንዳመን ለታይ

ከም ዝመስለኒ . . .
ሓበሻ ዝግኒ ምምረጸ ካብ ባኒ
ለታይ ሓበሻ ለሚዳ እንተትኸውን
ሰለፉ ኣይምጠዓመንዶ ዝግኒ?
ጣልያን ኢዩ ባኒኡ ዝፈቱ
ስለዚ ጣልያን ለሚዳ ለቲ ማለት'ዩ
ግን ከኣ እታ «ተቔነኒ»
ቁሩብ ኣሕሲባህኒ ኣደናጊራህኒ
ትፈልጥዋ እንተኼንኩም
ኣብዚኣስ ምደለኹ ሓገዝኩም
ማርያም ትሓግዝኩም!

The Learned

The learned have brains
Enough to say *I don't know.*
I've made a mistake.
Please explain.
I don't understand.
They say
Better to savor questions
And argue pro and con
Than to spit out answers
Not your own.
They also warn
Against the learned who claim
To make knowledge into religion
And cry *Believe! Believe!*
Forgetting that to be learned
Is to have only one first name:
Skeptic.

ምሁር

ምሁር'ዩ ሓንጎል ኣሎዎ
ኣይፈልጥን ዝብል እንተዘይፈሊጡዎ
ተጋግየ ዝብል እንተ ስሒቱዎ
ኣረድኡኒ ግለጹዎ! ግለጹዎ!

ምሁር ይብል . . .
እንኩ ሕቶ ባዕልኹም መልሱዎ
ርኣዩዎ ስምዑዎ ዳህስሱዎ
ፈትኑዎ እንደገና ፈትኑዎ
ሞጉትኩም ተማጉትኩም ርትዑዎ
መዚንኩም ፈሊጥኩም እተውዎ

ንዝብለኩም . . .
እመኑዎ! እመኑዎ! እመኑዎ!
ነቲ ፍልጠት ሃይማኖት ጌሩዎ
ይግባይ ብሉ ወጥሩዎ
ሓዝዎ ሰተት ከይተብሉዎ
ንምሁር እኮ ምሁር ኣሎዎ።

Dear Africans

The overweight
God, America,
Is always late.
Don't wait.

You already know
What he'll state:
*I regret the hearsay
Of so many dead and dying
And so much crying.*

You already know
What he'll think:
*It's dress-down Friday.
Can we have a snack?
Oh, man! Make that a big Mac
And a large Coke.
By the way, don't smoke.*

ኣመሪካ ኢሉኩም

ዝሞተ እንተ ሞተ
ንዑ ኮላ ንስተ
ዝብላዕ ዘይብልኩም
እንሆልኩም ማንካ
ዝሽመት ዘይብልኩም
እንሆልኩም ባንካ
ዘሎኩም ነጊፍኩም
ኩሉ ንዓይ ኣመሪካ

ናብራ ከሎኩም
ናብራ ተለቂሕኩም
ናብራ ከሎኩም
ናብራ ተገዚእኩም
ናብራ ከሎኩም
ናብራ ለሚንኩም
ኣነ ክጽውዕ
ኣቤት እንዳበልኩም
ናጽነት ሓርነት
እንታይ ክገብረልኩም

ነዚ ዘይኣመንኩም
ብረት ክሽጠልኩም
እንተ ብህይወትኩም
እንተ ብሞትኩም
ክኽስበኩም 'የ
ኣፍሪቃውያን።።

Exile

Ethiopian women
Who are gorgeous
And wearing traditional dress
Wait in Cairo airport:
Beirut bound export
For restless lives
Of making beds
And little money.
Go with God, my beauties.
I don't envy you.

ስደት

ኣብ ካይሮ ኤርፖርት
ዙርያ ዝለበሳ
ገለ ሓሙሳ ሱሳ
ልቢ ዝማርኻ
ልቢ ዘፍስሳ
ርእናየን ናይ ኢትዮጵያ ኤክስፖርት
ንበይሩት ክሓልፋ
ናይ ሰብ ዓራት ከንጽፋ
ህይወተን ከሕልፋ
ክንደይ ከይህብትማ ክንደይ ከየዕርፋ
ይኹነልክን ይቕናዕክን በላ ሕለፋ
ነዚኣስ ኣይንደልያ ኣይንሃርፋ።

Empty Handed

I came home a millionaire.
Let's feast! Drink
And be merry!
Huh? Mom? Dad? What?

Time to wake up
In the name of the Father,
The Son and the Holy Spirit.
There's not enough to eat.

Yesterday like today and tomorrow,
I only want to go home,
But empty handed?

እንታይ ሒዘ

ሕልሚ ሓሊመ
ሚልዮናት ተሸኪመ
ዓደይ ድርግም
ኣውርዱ ሳርማ
ሕረዱ ጮማ
ኣዕልሉ'ቦ ኣዕልሊ ማማ!
ብርር እንተበልኩዓ
በስመ ኣብ ወልደ መንፈስ ቅዱስ
ንኣፈይ ዘይከፎ'ነኩዓ . . .
ሎሚ ጽባሕ! ሎሚ ጽባሕ!
ክምለስ ደስ ምበለኒ ባህ
እንታይ ሒዘ?

Outside

I have my people
Outside
And many things:
Underwear, pants,
Shirt, tie,
Socks, shoes,
Watch, my shades and scarf,
I got them all outside
And today I'm not suffering.
Tomorrow, who knows?

ወጻኢ

አሎወሪኒ አብ ወጻኢ
አሎኒ ናይ ወጻኢ
ሙታንተይ ናይ ወጻኢ
ካናቴራይ ናይ ወጻኢ
ስረይ ናይ ወጻኢ
ካምቻይ ናይ ወጻኢ
ጃካይ ናይ ወጻኢ
ክራቫታይ ናይ ወጻኢ
ካልሰይ ናይ ወጻኢ
ሰዓተይ ናይ ወጻኢ
አኪያለይ ናይ ወጻኢ
መንዲለይ ከማን ናይ ወጻኢ
አነ'ዶ ሎሚ ክውጻዕኢ
እግዚሄር ይፈልጥ ናይ መጻኢ!

Quhaito

Stones, who carved you?
Statues, who made you stand?
Houses, who made you homes?

Quhaito,
Who smashed the pots,
Battered you down
And ploughed you under?

Ancient times,
Open your belly of earth
And give birth
To the alphabet and paint
Of old loves and hates.

Quhaito, utter the name:
Who dammed the water at Safra
To flow then and now?
Are times the same

Between the blossoming aloes
And tahbeb flowers for honey,
With blood red barley
Overrunning your rich plains?

Can you tell me
The bishop of your monastery,
Cold and high
Between the sea and sky?

ቄሓይቶ ንል ድሮ

ቄሓይቶ ንል ድሮ
አእማንኪ መን ወቸሮ
ሓወልትኺ መን ኮመሮ
አባይትኺ መን ሰፈሮ ነበሮ

መንከ'ፍረሰ መን ቀበሮ
መን ኮን ይኾውን ሰባር ዕትሮ

ይውጽአልኪ ንል ቀደም
ናይ ቀደም ፍቕሪ
ናይ ቀደም ደም
ናይ ቀደም ፈደል
ናይ ቀደም ቀለም
አብ ከብድኺ ዝሓዝክዮ ዓለም

ተዛረቢ ቄሓይቶ
ማይ ሳፍራ መን ኺዓቶ

ሎሚ ድዩ ቀደም
ሎሚ ከም ቀደም
ዕምባባ ምጸ ምጸ
ዕምባባ ታሀበብ
ደም ዝሰረበ ስገም
ለምለም ዝባንኪ ዝበሓቶ

ምቕማጥኪ ገምገም ባሕሪ
ጥቓ ሰማይ ልዕሊ ምድሪ
ጥቓ ጸሓይ እሞ ቄሪ
አነስ ምበልኩኺ ደብሪ
መን አቡንኪ እስከ ዘክሪ።

The War Makes Sense

Play it again.
Adam's and Eve's children,
Brothers and sisters,
We carry their one name

We laugh and cry the same.
We die and live again.

Who's Abel? Who's Cain?
We'll know the difference.

ክንፋለጥ ኢና

ደቂ ኣዳም እንዲና
ደቂ ሄዋን እንዲና
እስከ ንበል ኣሕዋት ኢና
ሓደ'ቦና ሓንቲ'ዴና

ህይወቶም ህይወትና
ሓጎሶም ሓጎስና
ሓዘኖም ሓዘንና
ሞቶም ሞትና

እስከ ንበል ቀሪብና ኢና
ኣቤል መኒና
ቃኤል መኒና
ክንፋለጥ ኢና

Meat

Like Lions,
Humble tigers
Or just plain cats
We want meat.
Forget your vegetables.

Meat,
Innards and bones at least:
Cut fresh, dried,
Chicken, hot *injera* . . .
We tear it apart
Forget your vegetables.

Barley beer, honey wine, arak —
Don't be cheap.
Fill it up.
Grrrrrr-eat!
Let's eat meat

Like lions. Too much?
Call us tigers
Or just plain cats.
Give us meat.
Forget your vegetables.

ስጋና ሃብና

አናብስ እንዲና
አናብር ምስ ትሕትና
ደማሙ እንተሓመ'ኽና
ስጋና ሃብና ስጋና
ሓምሊ ድአ እንታይ ክገብረልና

ሕሙቶ ዝግኒ ዓጽሚ
ግዕዝም ጥብሲ ቄልዋ
ዝልዝል ቋንጣ
ደርሆ
ምስ ጣይታ ብውዕይታ

ዝስተ ሃብና ወርቂ
ስዋ ሜስ አረቒ
አቲ ክንደይ ትበቒ
መልእዩ 'ባ
ሕ..ጇ ድንቒ

አናብስ እንዲና
አናብር ምስ ትሕትና
ደማሙ እንተሓመ'ኽና
ስጋና ሃብና ስጋና
ሓምሊ ድአ እንታይ ክገብረልና

To Rome

"Come to Rome
And play your poems,
Z-ezm, b-ebum,
And sing your Tigrinya.
Dress in your *gabi*
And share who you are."

So, Rome invites me
To read my poetry.
Do I need my flywhisk?

One hundred years
After making us a colony
And reading the chronicles of our culture
By Conti Rossini
And later the teachings of Padre Gasparini
Rome finally listens
And hears

The voice of Eritrea
In the poetry and children.

Now Rome wants me.
Of course, I go.
But don't I need my flywhisk?

ሮማ

እቲ ሮማ
ጭራይ ዶ ክማልአ
ፈውሲ ሃመማ

በሉ ኸይደ ንሮማ
ንሳ'ያ ዓዲማ
ንዓ ኢላትኒ ንዓ በኛኻ
እስክሉ ኢላትኒ እስክሉ ግጥምኻ
እስክሉ ኢላትኒ እስክሉ ጋቢኻ
እስክሉ ኢላትኒ እስክሉ ባህልኻ
እስክሉ ትጽበየኒ'ላ ተሃዊኻ

ብኮንቲ ሮሲኒ ተሓቢራ ኔራ
በ'ባ ጋስፓሪኒ ተሓቢራ ኔራ
ንዓይና ድእ'ምበር እዝናስ ዓዊራ
አይሰምዓቶን ኔራ ግጥሚ ናይ ኤርትራ
አይሰምዓቶን ኔራ ካብ ደቂ ኤርትራ

እቲ ሮማ
ጭራይ ዶ ክማልአ
ፈውሲ ሃመማ

Meskerem

Nature loves all twelve
Sisters who join our year,
Especially Spring,
And she takes me.

Who is she? Where?
How can I compare
Love's immeasurable,
Invisible first cause
With someone tall or short,
Dark or light?
I only say, "Meskerem,"

And feel the effects of her power:
The world in ecstasy
With Meskerem in the meadows
Like a strong drink of honey.

Sky, no more tears.
Earth, meet the sun
And prepare to feast.
We are the guests.

Come, creatures, come.
Come day and night.
We've had the grains and fruits
And all the vegetable soup,
But now the meat and butter.

Come, children.
Chew some cane
With your runny noses.

መስከረም

ካብ ኣሕዋታ ብሕብረት
መፍቶ ኩሉ ፍጥረት
መስከረም'ያ ሸማ
ልበይ ዝማረኽት

መስከረም'ያ እዚ ኩሉ ትገብር
ካብ መን ትነውሕ ካብ መን ትሓጽር
ካብ መን ትቐይሕ ካብ መን ትጥቅር
መን ርእዮዋ ኣበይ ትነብር
ኣነ ዝፈልጣ ዓለም ከተስክር ብመስተንኽር

ሰማይ ሆየ ገዲፉዋ ም'ብካይ
መሬት ሆየ ተዓጢቓ ውራይ
ኣቱም ፍጥረት ውዓሉ እንዶ ምሳይ
ኣብዛ ጽሓይ ከ'ቐርበልኩም ሸሻይ
ሰዊት ተኽሊ ሰዊት እኽሊ ግባት ዳሕራይ

ነቶም ቆልዑ ነፋጣት ኣፍንጫ
እንኩ እስከ ብልዑ ብልዑ ቃንጫ

በዓል ዕምባባ መን ከማይ
ሓሪር ተኸዲነን ናባይ ናባይ
ንዓ ንህቢ ንዒ ጭሩ ንዑ ንፈሩ
ኣይትሕፈሩ ድላይኩም ግበሩ

Weaver birds and bees,
Come fly.
No one can be shy.

Brides under gauzy gowns,
Their hems and necklines striped
Gold, red, blue and green,
Come into the streets
For young men with torches
Of twigs and songs like
"Hoyé-hoyé, Hoyé-hoyé —
Forget being old, forget sleep
For the fresh greens, birth, milk
And Meskerem with her butter . . . ."

First born and the new in every year,
Who is she? Where? My love?
I only know her shadow
But feel the world in ecstasy
With Meskerem in the meadows.

እተን መርዑ ተኸዲነን ዙርያ
ወርቂ ቀይሕ ሰማያዊ ቀጠልያ
ገዘአን ገዲፈን ንግዳም ንጽርግያ
ምስቶም አጉባዝ ተሸኪሞም ሸሸግ
ሆየ ሆየ ሃየ አይንባዕግግ
መስከረም መጺአ ጠሲሚ ንዝብሀግ

መስከረም ቦኹሪ ዓመታ
ፈትየያ 'ሉኹ ብጽላሎታ
ሂቢያ ዶኹን ዘይናታ
አየ እንተዝረኸባ ብህይወታ
መስ መስከረም መስከር ዓለም . . . አነስ ናታ!